My First Book of BIBLE VERSES

Susan Jones

Love one another,
as I have loved you.

—JOHN 15:12

Good Books
New York, New York

Good Books books may be purchased in bulk at special discounts for sales promotion, corporate gifts, fund-raising, or educational purposes. Special editions can also be created to specifications. For details, contact the Special Sales Department, Good Books, 307 West 36th Street, 11th Floor, New York, NY 10018 or info@skyhorsepublishing.com.

Good Books is an imprint of Skyhorse Publishing, Inc.®, a Delaware corporation.

Visit our website at www.goodbooks.com.

10 9 8 7 6 5 4 3 2 1

Library of Congress Cataloging-in-Publication Data is available on file.

Cover design by Michele Trombley
Cover illustration used under license from Shutterstock.com.

Print ISBN: 978-1-68099-281-6
Ebook ISBN: 978-1-68099-289-2

Printed in China

How to Use This Book

It's never too early to learn about the Bible and its teachings. *My First Book of Bible Verses* is a fun way to introduce your little one to the beauty and meaning of God's word. Inside you'll find 30 inspiring Bible verses along with modern, kid-friendly explanations to help clarify the verses' meaning for children of all ages.

Begin by having your child listen as you read a cherished verse out loud. Encourage your little one to repeat the words along with you. Make learning fun: Be generous with your praise and give children plenty of chances to get the words just right. When a child succeeds in learning a verse by heart, he or she may choose a special sticker as a reward! Help them find the matching animal sticker on the enclosed sticker pages and cheer their efforts as they place it in the space provided. Depending on your child's age, consider introducing a new verse every week—soon they will be able to recite dozens of Bible verses by heart.

Don't forget to celebrate every one of your child's successes with a big hug and loving words of encouragement. Enjoy sharing elements of your faith each and every day and adding the comfort of God's love and guidance to your child's expanding world.

I have hidden your word in my heart that I might not sin against you.

–PSALM 119:11

In the beginning God created the heaven and the earth.

—GENESIS 1:1

Before God, there was nothing but darkness. It took God six days to add light to the world and create all the beautiful wonders in the sky above, in the oceans below, and here on land. On the seventh day, God rested.

The earth is the Lord's and all that is in it,
the world, and those who live in it.

—PSALM 24:1

God made the earth and all the
things on it: the trees, the flowers,
the animals, and the people! They
do not belong to us, but we must
take good care of them.

Thy word is a lamp unto my feet, and a light unto my path.

—PSALM 119:105

When we are lost in the dark, a lamp can help us find our way. The Bible is just like that lamp! It helps us make decisions and guides us like a light. When you need help making choices or finding your way in life, read the Bible and let God's word help you.

Wait on the Lord: be of good courage, and he shall strengthen thine heart.

—PSALM 27:14

When you are feeling sad or scared, be brave and trust that God will make you strong. God will always be there to help you when you need Him.

One God and Father of all, who is above all, and through all, and in you all.

—EPHESIANS 4:6

There is one God and He is very powerful. He is also a part of everything, including *you*, because He is the creator of everything.

Let all your things be done with charity.

—1 CORINTHIANS 16:14

"Charity" is another word for love. Allow God's love to overflow to those around you by sharing what you have with them and helping people in need. Whether you are playing on the swings or cleaning up your toys, do it with love in your heart!

... walk as children of light:
(For the fruit of the Spirit is in all
goodness and righteousness and truth;) ...

—EPHESIANS 5:8–9

When you trust God to be in charge of your life, it's like you are adopted into God's family! You start to see things differently, as if a light has been turned on. God's spirit will help you to be truthful and to do the right thing.

I will both lie down and sleep in peace;
for you alone, O Lord, make me lie
down in safety.

—PSALM 4:8

Every night you can sleep peacefully knowing that God is looking out for you and protecting you. Let His love wrap around you like a blanket.

Great peace have those who love your law, and nothing can make them stumble.

—PSALM 119:165

People who follow God's rules have joy and peace in their hearts. God gives them the power to face any problem in their lives.

Wait for the Lord; be strong and take heart and wait for the Lord.

—PSALM 27:14

Even on your worst day, you are not alone.
Be strong and wait for God to bring you comfort.
You can trust Him to always be there for you.

Give thanks to the Lord,
for He is good. His love
endures forever.

—PSALM 136:1

When people give you a gift, you say, *Thank you.*
Don't forget to do the same for God. His kindness and
forgiveness are gifts that He is always ready to give.

When I am afraid, I put my trust in you.

—PSALM 56:3

When you are afraid of something, try talking to God. It feels better to tell Him about your fears, even if it is difficult to say them out loud. Know that God loves you and wants what is best for you.

Set your affection on things above, not on things on the earth.

—COLOSSIANS 3:2

Toys and games and clothes are fun, but they
are not what we should care about most.
Only God can give us true joy and contentment.
His love and guidance are most important.

Welcome one another, therefore, just as Christ has welcomed you, for the glory of God.

—ROMANS 15:7

God loves us no matter who we are and has invited us to be part of His family. You can show other kids God's love by inviting them to join your games, saying hello, or even just smiling warmly.

Bear one another's burdens, and in this way you will fulfill the law of Christ.

—GALATIANS 6:2

Jesus says, "A new command I give you: Love one another. As I have loved you, so you must love one another" (John 13:34). Loving someone means caring about them and helping them when they need it. When we help each other, we are keeping Jesus's commandment to love one another.

Do not judge, so that you may not be judged.

—MATTHEW 7:1

When other people make mistakes or get in trouble, it's easy to make fun or gossip. The truth is that we all make mistakes. God loves everyone, even when we mess up, and only He knows what's really going on in our hearts. Only God can judge.

Let your light so shine before men, that they may see your good works, and glorify your Father which is in heaven.

—MATTHEW 5:16

Every time you do a good deed with a loving attitude, you shine like a light for all to see God's love. When you help someone, share your toys, or are kind, you are showing those around you a little bit of God's goodness.

Be devoted to one another in love.
Honor one another above yourselves.

—ROMANS 12:10

Treat other people like they are part of your family: respect them and love them like you respect and love your own family.

Honor your father and your mother, so that your days may be long in the land that the Lord your God is giving you.

—EXODUS 20:12

God says that you should respect and honor your parents. When you are a kid, honoring your parents means being thankful for them and obeying their rules.

In everything do to others as you
would have them do to you . . .

—MATTHEW 7:12

Treat others the way you would want them to treat you. Do you like it when people share with you? Then share with other people! Do you like it when kids invite you to play with them? Then invite other kids to play with you!

Jesus answered, "I am the way and the truth and the life. No one comes to the Father except through me."

—JOHN 14:6

Because of Jesus's life and His death on the cross, we can have a wonderful relationship with God! There's no other way to be close to God except through Jesus.

He said to him, "'You shall love the Lord your God with all your heart, and with all your soul, and with all your mind."

—MATTHEW 22:37

Jesus is reminding His listeners of the rules that God gave Moses to share with God's people way back in the Old Testament times (Deuteronomy 6:5). Jesus says that if we love God completely, all the other rules God gives us—to be kind to each other, to honor our parents, to be honest, and others—will be easy to follow! Sometimes we love ourselves more than we love God, and then we start breaking God's rules.

This is my commandment, That ye love one another as I have loved you.

—JOHN 15:12

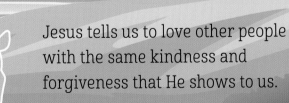

Jesus tells us to love other people with the same kindness and forgiveness that He shows to us.

Every good and perfect
gift is from above . . .

—JAMES 1:17

All the good things in life come from God. Let's thank God for the gifts He gives us—from the earth and the trees, to friends and family. What gifts do you want to thank God for today?

A friend loveth at all times,
and a brother is born for adversity.

—PROVERBS 17:17

True friends and family are the ones who will always be there to help you and protect you, even during hard times. Treat these people like treasures, and ask God to help you be the best friend and family member that you can be.

We love because he first loved us.

—1 JOHN 4:19

We know how to love other people because God taught us by His example. He even sent down His son, Jesus, to save us with His love.

When you search for me, you will find me;
if you seek me with all your heart.

—JEREMIAH 29:13

God loves us and wants to have a relationship with each one of us. When we look for God, we may not be able to see him with our eyes, but He will always be available to guide and help us.

The Lord is good to all, and
his compassion is over all
that he has made.

—PSALM 145:9

God loves all of His creation—each
person, flower, animal, and tree—
everything He has made. He cares
deeply about the whole world.

Pray without ceasing.

—1 THESSALONIANS 5:17

God is a wonderful friend. You can pray to God anytime, anywhere. You can even pray silently in your heart and God will hear you! We can't always be kneeling by our beds, talking to God, of course, but we can always have an attitude of gratitude and trust in God.

Trust in the Lord forever,
for in the Lord God you have
an everlasting rock.

—ISAIAH 26:4

Rocks are big and difficult to move. So is God: He does not budge. You can try to push Him away, but He will not go. He's like a rock that you can always lean on.